Be Your Own Boss

Small Businesses

ERNESTINE GIESECKE

Heinemann Library
Chicago, Illinois

Designed by Herman Adler Design
Photo research by John Klein
Printed and bound in China by Leo Paper Group Manufacturing, Inc.

09
10 9 8 7 6 5 4

Library of Congress Cataloging-in-Publication Data
Giesecke, Ernestine, 1945-
  Be your own boss : small businesses / Ernestine Giesecke.
    p. cm. — (Everyday economics)
Summary: Describes the characteristics of small businesses, why many people find them attractive, and how to start and manage a small business.
Includes bibliographical references and index.
  ISBN: 978-1-58810-493-9 (1-58810-493-1) (HC)
  ISBN: 978-1-58810-956-9 (1-58810-956-9) (Pbk)
1. Small business—Management—Juvenile literature.
2. New business enterprises—Juvenile literature.
3. Entrepreneurship—Juvenile literature. [1. Small business—Management. 2. Entrepreneurship. 3. Business—Vocational guidance. 4. Vocational guidance.]
I. Title. II. Series.
  HD62.5 .G53 2002
  658.02'2—dc21
                                    2002013702

Acknowledgments
The author and publisher are grateful to the following for permission to reproduce copyright material:
Cover photograph by ImageBank/Getty Images.
Title page, pp. 11, 15, 19, 31, 40 National Foundation for Teaching Entrepreneurship; p.4 Robert Brenner/PhotoEdit; p. 4 George Nikitin/AP Wide World Photos; p. 7TL Stone/Getty Images; pp. 7TR, 7B Reuters NewMedia Inc./Corbis; p. 7C Bettman/CORBIS; p. 8 Jim Pickerell/Stock Connection/PictureQuest; p. 9 Mug Shots/The Stock Market/Corbis; p. 13 Darrell Eager Photography; p. 21 Corbis Images/PictureQuest; p. 22 Sue Gregory; p. 25 Doug Wilson/Cobis; p. 27 Mary F. Calvert/Washington Times; p. 29; p. 33 Jason Upshaw; p. 40L David Young-Wolff/PhotoEdit; p. 41C Dan Loh/AP Wide World Photos; p. 41R Amy Etra/PhotoEdit; p. 43 Susan Van Etten/PhotoEdit.

Every effort has been made to contact copyright holders of any material reproduced in this book. Any omissions will be rectified in subsequent printings if notice is given to the publisher.

Note to the Reader: Some words are shown in bold, **like this.** You can find out what they mean by looking in the glossary.

Contents

3

What Is a Small Business?

Nearly three-quarters of businesses in the United States do not have employees. In these small businesses, the owner does all the work.

Small businesses may include the "Mom and Pop" grocery store at the corner, the hair salon on the next block, and the automobile repair shop across from the bank. Each of these businesses may have less than five employees. The day care center across from the school may have only one employee; it, too, is a small business.

Know It

In general, a small business is a business that has less than 500 employees. This size standard was developed by the United States Small Business Administration.

Small businesses also may include the community bank, which has four branches, three drive-up locations, and a total of 400 employees. And, even though there are hundreds of pizza restaurants and sandwich shops with the same name and menu scattered across the country, each location acts as a small business.

Every year, thousands of new businesses open their doors. The **entrepreneurs** who start these businesses will work hard to make them successful.

Each of these businesses was started by an entrepreneur, a person who starts and owns his or her business. Entrepreneurs work for themselves and are responsible for the success—or failure—of the business. An entrepreneur hopes to make his or her business succeed by satisfying a consumer or market need.

The Small Business Administration (SBA), created in 1953, is an independent agency of the **federal** government. The SBA's goal is to aid, counsel, and protect the interests of small businesses.

The SBA's resources are available to any budding entrepreneur or small businessperson who needs help. The SBA operates a toll-free "Answer Desk" to give callers direct referral to appropriate sources of information. The agency also maintains a website designed to encourage teens and young adults to begin their own businesses.

Want a cookie?

Debbi Sivyer began baking cookies as a teenager. "Chocolate chip cookies were an easy project... just the thing to keep you busy on a rainy afternoon." After she married Randy Fields, she found that her husband's clients often asked that she bake for their visits. Debbi decided to go into the cookie business. In 1977, at the age of twenty, Debbi opened her first store. She sold $50 worth of cookies on her first day in business and $75 worth on her second day. Today, there are hundreds of company- and independently-owned Mrs. Fields' stores throughout the United States, as well as in several other countries.

Small Business and the Economy

Small businesses form the foundation of our **economy**. With only a few exceptions, each of America's large corporations grew from a small business. These businesses began small, then added employees as their sales and number of customers increased.

Small businesses make a huge contribution to the economy. For example, 99 out of 100 U.S. businesses are small businesses, employing less than 500 people. More than half the nation's workers are employed by small businesses. In 1998, those employees earned about $1.5 **trillion.** Perhaps more important is the effect small businesses have on job creation. Each year, small businesses create seven of every ten new jobs. In a recent year, small businesses created four million new jobs. During the same year, big businesses lost 1.7 million jobs.

Small **firms** employ more workers under age 25 and over age 65 than do large firms. Many of these employees work part-time and could not easily

Small business numbers

The Small Business Administration records show that small businesses:

Make up 99 percent of all U.S. businesses

Include 99.7 percent of all U.S. employers

Create about 75 percent of the nation's new jobs each year

Employ about 53 percent of the private workforce

Contribute 47 percent of all sales in the country

Small business inventions

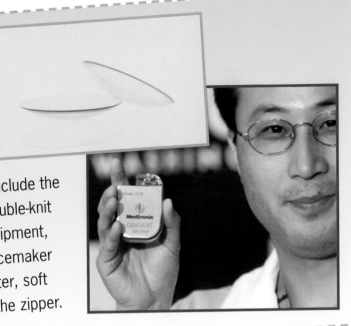

In the past 100 years, small businesses have been the source of many new products and inventions. Some of these include the airplane, audiotape recorder, double-knit fabric, fiber-optic examining equipment, heart valve, optical scanner, pacemaker (right bottom), personal computer, soft contact lenses (right top), and the zipper.

fit into a large corporation. Small firms often provide the first job experience for most people. Furthermore, small firms offer employees the opportunity to fill many different roles within the company.

Another feature of small businesses is their **flexibility**. Small businesses are often willing to try something new. They are responsible for developing new ideas, new products, and new ways of doing business. In addition, small businesses can survive with fewer customers. This allows small businesses to offer specialized **services** and products that would be too costly for a large corporation to offer.

One of today's largest companies, General Electric, can be traced back to 1892 and the small business started by Thomas Edison. Today, General Electric employs about 313,000 people.

In 1984, Michael Dell, aged nineteen, started a small computer company. Today, Dell Computers employs about 34,400 people.

Why Start a Small Business?

People have many different reasons for starting their own business. Most say they enjoy the feeling of accomplishment that comes with starting and running their own business. **Entrepreneurs** enjoy planning the business and watching it grow, all the while realizing that they made it happen. Many say that the sense of pride and fulfillment is more rewarding than money.

Some entrepreneurs find that sharing their hobby can lead to a **profit**-making business. For example, collecting sports cards—baseball, hockey, or basketball—can lead to a business in buying, trading, and selling cards. A card, which sells for $1.00 this year, may sell for $3.50 in two or three years. In this case, the entrepreneur gets to enjoy his or her hobby and make money at the same time!

A recent survey indicated that 72 percent of working people say they are mistreated at work. Even more surprising is that 42 percent of working people greatly dislike their jobs.

Occasionally, young people use the experience they gain at a **minimum-wage** summer job as a springboard to their own business. A teen may take a minimum-wage summer job at a print shop that does some desktop publishing. The teen can use the job to learn as much as possible about that part of the business. The next year, the teen may have enough experience to start a small desktop publishing business and work with small companies to create flyers, newsletters, and advertising **brochures.** Often, a self-employed teen can earn twice as much as a teen working for someone else.

Some young people start their businesses in order to gain hands-on experience they can use later in life. And, because young entrepreneurs risk relatively little money, they can use both their successes and their failures to learn about what skills and qualities are needed to be successful in starting and running a business.

Finally, some people work at their own business because they can control their working environment. This means that they are responsible for making themselves happy in their jobs.

Cards, cards, cards. . .

David Leopold started a trading card business when he was thirteen years old. David loves sports and had collected several thousand baseball cards. When the cards began to take up too much room, he decided to sell them. He found that the cards were worth more than three times what he paid for them! Cards that are rare, players that are popular, and a player's success work together to increase a card's value. Often, the card showing the player as a rookie is the most valuable.

Leopold decided to start a business. In four years, his business, D & L Collectibles, had between 400,000 and 500,000 cards with an annual budget of about $6,500.

Who Starts a Small Business?

There are no secrets to running a small business—nearly everyone who wants to, can. There are, however, some particular characteristics that help small business owners succeed.

Here are some questions to help you decide if you have what it takes to own and manage a small business.

Know It

Few people start a business with all of the basic skills needed. A business owner should know what areas represent strengths and what areas represent weaknesses. Even more important, a wise business owner knows where and when to go for help.

Are you a self-starter?

As the owner of a small business, you must constantly be alert and ready to do any task that needs attention. You'll need to put effort into starting a business. And, you'll need to put just as much effort into keeping the business going. Playing hooky is not allowed!

Do you get along with a variety of personalities?

As the owner and operator of a business, you will need to work with a wide range of clients, customers, and suppliers. You may have to deal with unpleasant customers or rude suppliers. Establishing good working relations with everyone will help insure the success of your business.

Are you good at making decisions?

A business owner must be able to accurately understand and evaluate each problem or opportunity the business presents. Sometimes there is little time available to make a decision that can have a great effect on the business.

These young people received awards from NFTE for writing excellent business plans.

Two traits necessary for successful **entrepreneurs** are creativity and **innovation**. In addition, successful entrepreneurs share some personality traits and characteristics. Among these traits are persistence, goal-oriented behavior, strong drive to achieve, high energy level, independence, problem-solving skills, reliability, organization, adaptability, and tolerance of failure.

Do you have the physical and emotional strength to run a business?

A new business may need attention every working hour for days at a time. A business owner must be able to keep going in the face of roadblocks and disappointments.

Do you plan and organize efficiently?

To keep the business running smoothly, you'll need to look ahead. For example, you'll need to be sure you have enough supplies and **raw materials**. It's important that you put aside enough money to pay **wages** and taxes before the due dates arrive.

Do you have enough drive to stay interested in the business?

If you lose interest in a hobby within a month or two, starting a business may not be right for you. Starting and maintaining a business requires a **long-term** commitment.

Choosing a Business

All businesses fall into four basic categories: manufacturing, wholesale, retail, and **service**. A manufacturing company makes a product, such as skateboards or computers. A wholesale business buys products in large quantities from manufacturers and then sells smaller quantities of the products to retailers. A retail business buys products from wholesalers and sells them directly to consumers. A service business provides a service, such as dog grooming, website design, or automobile detailing, to customers.

To start a business, you need a great idea. The idea may come from work, school, hobbies, or potential customers. Most often, the best business for you will be in an area in which you are skilled and interested. Once you begin to think about a particular business, check with local businesspeople to find out if it is a business that can grow.

Know It

According to the National Foundation for Teaching **Entrepreneurship** (NFTE, pronounced "nifty"), the three most popular ideas among teens for starting a business include:
- reselling fashion, everything from jewelry to T-shirts;
- baked goods, such as pies or cakes; and
- building computer hardware.

When you are thinking about what to do for your own business, it may help to learn about products and services already available. For example, you might visit some well-known company Internet sites such as the Walt Disney Company, Binney & Smith, or Wham-O. List three favorite things about the site and three ideas for your product or service.

Computer fixing

One Minneapolis, Minnesota, fifth grader's business began when he had to stay home from school with a sore throat. Trent Eisenberg kept himself busy with his computer—not playing games, but taking the computer apart. Then he figured out how to put it back together again!

When he was fourteen, he posted a fix for a computer problem online in a computer chatroom. The next day, a company representative e-mailed Eisenberg, offering him a job with the computer company. That prompted Eisenberg to start F1 Computers.

At seventeen, Eisenberg's customers—adults with a variety of careers—turned to him for help repairing or installing their systems. His business has grown and within three years it brought in more than $50,000 a year. Eisenberg intends to use the money from his business to pay for college.

Some people find that they can turn their hobby into a business. This choice has a built-in advantage. Because they enjoy the business, business owners do not mind working hard to make the business successful.

Many people find they would prefer to start a business that offers services rather than one which manufactures or sells a product. In order to manufacture items, an entrepreneur has to buy the **raw materials** needed to make the product. If the business is selling products, the business must first make or buy the items to resell.

Service businesses, however, do not require the purchase of raw materials. In a service business, an entrepreneur does physical or mental work for his or her clients. Work such as computer programming, car washing, grass cutting, and house painting are popular services.

What Do I Need?

When **entrepreneurs** begin to turn a business dream into a reality, they often have the drive, desire, and talent. Then they begin to make lists of the things they will need—**raw materials**, space to work, tools, price tags, etc. The list is different for each business. Even a **service** business will need office supplies and a telephone.

However, every new business needs one thing to start—a business plan. A business plan is a document that defines your business and identifies its goals. To prepare a business plan, an entrepreneur will need to investigate and research the business he or she plans to start. A business plan is like a road map. It helps you see where you are, where you want to go, and how you plan to get there.

A business plan answers the following questions:
- What kind of business is this?
- What service or product does the business provide?
- Who will buy the service or product?
- Who is the **competition?**
- What is the sales **strategy?**
- How will the work get done?
- Who will do the work?
- How much money is needed to start the businesses?
- How soon will the business provide a **profit?**

While one business plan may be different from another, nearly all business plans include an introduction, or summary, and sections describing the company, the market, the products and services offered by the company, the company's sales strategy, its **finances**, and its management and operations. In some cases, additional information is included in an appendix.

Research shows that a business plan is a "must have" for a small business. A survey by AT&T states that more than half of the small businesses that succeed started with a business plan. In general, small companies with business plans have 50 percent more **revenue** and profit growth than companies without a plan.

The National Foundation for Teaching Entrepreneurship

The National Foundation for Teaching Entrepreneurship (NFTE) was created to teach entrepreneurship to low-income young people, between ages eleven and eighteen. Each year, NFTE sponsors a business plan competition for new businesses and for businesses less than a year old. Prize money goes toward each winner's business or college education.

Business Plan: Introduction

The first few pages of your business plan should provide a reader with an **overview** of your business. Wise **entrepreneurs** use the question, "What business am I in?" as a guide when writing this section. Identify the business's products, market, and **services**. Explain what makes the business unique.

A business plan's introduction should accomplish the following:

- Give a general description of the business.
- Explain the type of business.
- Discuss the products and services offered.
- Discuss the advantages the business will have over the **competition**.
- Detail the ownership of the business.
- List the skills and experience you bring to the business.

Because it is the first thing a reader sees, the introduction, or summary, is one of the most important parts of the business plan.

dog biscuits Recipe

Business
Bake and sell preservative-free cookies and treats for dogs.

Owners
Susan Hanover and Tianna Madison ninth grade students at Westlake High School

Skills/Experience
Susan - baking experience
Tianna - sales experience

Advantage
fresh-baked cookies at several locations

Summary

Barker's Biscuits will specialize in homemade, preservative-free cookies, biscuits, treats, and bagels for dogs. Its founders, Miss Susan Hanover and Miss Tianna Madison are ninth grade students at Westlake High School. Barker's Biscuits will offer dog owners a chance to give their dogs treats that are fresh, preservative-free, and tasty. Unlike other currently available specialty biscuits, Barker's Biscuits will concentrate on the health benefits of the biscuits. Further, Barker's Biscuits will be sold at several outlets in the community.

Business plan tips

A title page helps give the business plan a professional look.

A table of contents will help the reader locate specific sections in your business plan.

A summary of a business plan should be short, yet contain enough detail to interest a reader, such as a banker. Leave out details that will be presented later in the business plan.

Write the plan so that it can be read quickly and easily. One way to make a plan easy to read is to place only one or two ideas on a page.

Listing important parts of the plan in outline or bullet form will help make the plan easy to read.

Use graphs or charts whenever possible. They help give a business plan a professional look.

Business Plan
for
Barker's Biscuits

2100 East Lake Street
Roscoe, Illinois 60657
(312) 555-1234

Susan Hanover
1422 Oak Street
Roscoe, Illinois
(312) 555-1234

Tianna Madison
1426 Main Street
Roscoe, Illinois
(312) 555-2369

January 15, 2002

Table of Contents

Executive Summary

Barker's Biscuits will specialize in homemade, preservative-free cookies, biscuits, treats, and bagels for dogs.

Its founders, Miss Susan Hanover and Miss Tianna Madison are ninth grade students at Westlake High School.

Barker's Biscuits will offer dog owners a chance to give their dogs treats that are fresh, preservative-free, and tasty. Unlike other currently available specialty biscuits, Barker's Biscuits will concentrate on the health benefits of the biscuits. Further, Barker's Biscuits will be sold at several outlets in the community.

Barker's keys to success include:

- Awareness of the added value associated with healthful foods and snacks for pets.
- Willingness to search for and obtain the highest quality ingredients at the lowest possible price.
- Distributing product in an area not yet served by a competitor.
- Offering flavors unavailable from national brand.
- Great affection and respect for our canine companions.

Barker's Biscuits has set reasonable short- and long-term goals.

- Sales of $ 2,000 in 2003 and $4,000 in 2004.
- Gross margin (cost per unit ÷ total sales) higher than 60
- Net income more than 10 % of sales by third year.

Barker's Biscuits projected sales

Sales in dollars

14000
12000
10000
8000
6000
4000
2000
0

Business Plan: The Market

Marketing

Barker's Biscuits aims to take advantage of three distinct market trends.

✓ The number of dogs in Roscoe has doubled in the last three years.

✓ Nation-wide, the amount of money spent on their pets has been steadily increasing, reaching more than $20 billion a year.

✓ Pet owners want to give their pets the best possible food, including human-grade and organic products.

Handwritten notes: Find out amount of money spent on pets

Search Internet – Keyword: pet spending

Recipe card: dog biscuits Recipe

The marketing section should tell whether or not the market is growing. Use information from statistics and surveys to back up your description of the market.

Before you start a business, you will need to do some market research. That is, you will need to know who will buy your product or who will use your **service**. Show a sample product to several people and find out what they think of the product. Ask if there is

Researching the **competition** can help you form your marketing plan. Questions such as these are useful:

- Who are your nearest direct competitors?
- How are your competitor's businesses doing?
- What can you learn from your competition's **operations** and advertising?
- How does your product or service differ from that of your competition?

something about the product they would change. If your business offers a service, ask friends and potential customers whether or not they would use the service. Most importantly, find out how much they would be willing to pay for a product or service like the one you describe.

After the market research is complete, you will want to plan how to market your business. Marketing can offer a way to organize your business. In general, there are four basic parts to marketing. They are known as the four P's:

- Product—what your business sells
- Price—what you will charge
- Promote—how you will tell the market about your business
- Provide—how you will get your product to the customer.

How well your business grows may depend in large part upon how you advertise your product or service. Make sure that your advertising is well planned. Be sure to set enough money aside to advertise effectively.

The Box Guys

It was Chris Borchardt's concern for the environment that led to the idea for The Box Guys. He noticed that there was a great amount of cardboard being buried in landfills. Chris convinced a moving company to pick up the cardboard and sell it to recyclers.

When he realized that many boxes could be reused, he began selling them to people who were planning to move. Chris now partners with realtors and moving companies to secure new business.

"By being a successful **entrepreneur,** I hope that I can inspire other young people to follow their dreams without fear of failure."

Business Plan: Products and Services

The products and **services** section of the business plan can address two of the P's of marketing: product and price.

Think about how you got your idea and why it will be a success. Be sure the plan tells whether your business is manufacturing, wholesaling, retail, or service. State clearly what your business is offering for sale.

The product and services section is the place for a specific list of products or services you will offer. Tell exactly what your product or service will be and how much it will cost.

dog biscuits

Recipe

dog park / party location

Products

Barker's Bakery will offer dog owners a fresh, wholesome, and preservative-free alternative to commercially produced dog treats.

✓ Barker's offers wheat-free treats to reduce allergic reactions.

✓ Flavors include dog favorites such as cheese and peanut butter.

✓ Baker's Biscuits cost $.50 a piece or $4.95 a dozen (approx. 8 oz.)

Services

Barker's will plan and run special-event parties for 4–12 dogs.

Services include invitations; decorations; organized games, activities, and competitions; and of course, treats.

events will be held at the owner's home or Wiggleyville Dog Park.

kaged events begin at $80/4 dogs. Price quotes for om events are available.

Make certain that the product or service you describe matches the information you presented in the market section of your plan. Who is your target market? That is, to whom do you hope to sell your product? What does the market want that your product or service will provide? Be sure to describe how your product or service meets market demands and fits market trends.

Too much work

A specific list of products or services may save you from a business that will not work. For example, two teens considered starting a wallpapering business. The weekend home improvement programs made it look easy! They started a list of what was involved: remove old wallpaper, sand and patch walls, match patterns, make edges meet in corners and along ceilings, keep wet paper wrinkle-free, etc. After checking their list, they decided that the wallpapering business would be too difficult, especially because some of the work had to be done on ladders. So, the teens looked for another new business idea.

Describe any feature of your business that offers an advantage over your **competition**. What do you do better than the competition? What makes your product or service one-of-a-kind? If there is no competition for your product or service, be sure to say so.

Business Plan: Sales

This section deals with the two remaining P's of marketing: promote and provide. Record your business's sales goals in this part of the business plan. The goals should be specific and they should be measurable. That is, you should be able to compare the business's performance to the business's goals and determine how the business is doing.

For example, your business might have a **short-term** sales goal of $400 a month at the end of the first six months. A check of the total sales for the sixth months of business will indicate if the business is on track. A **long-term** goal might be to expand the business to include Internet sales within five years.

Know It

Every business needs clear goals. A successful business frequently compares performance to goals to insure that the business is on the right track.

Warm wrists

Ten-year-old K-K Gregory liked to play in the snow outside her home in Bedford, Massachusetts. But she did not like the way her wrists got cold when snow slipped between her gloves and jacket sleeve. So, she sewed together a tube of fleece fabric to go around her wrist. To keep it from sliding up, she made a thumbhole in the tube. Even before she had a business, Gregory had a marketing idea. She made a dozen of the wrist warmers for her Girl Scout troop to try. A father of a troop member put Gregory and her mom in touch with a **patent** attorney to **trademark** her "Wristies." Gregory now counts FedEx and McDonald's among her customers.

Sales

Barker's Biscuits will be sold at specialty pet stores and sampled at veterinary clinics.

✓ Barker's Biscuits will be available at A Dog Named Sue, Barker and Meowski, and The Golden Fireplug.

✓ Bloom Animal Hospital, Family Pet Clinic, and NorthEast Vet Center have agreed to distribute product samples for three months.

✓ Barker's Biscuits are packaged in 8 ounce and 16 ounce brown paper bags with windows, and labeled with Barker's Biscuits logo and telephone number.

Be sure your business plan explains how your product or service is different from your competitors' products.

Keeping track of the competition is important to a business's sales **strategy**. If you know the competition, you can make your sales materials stand out.

Describe how your business will get your product or **service** to the customer. Indicate how the business will reach new customers and how it will encourage repeat customers.

This is the place in the business plan to indicate if sales of your product will change with the time of year. For instance, will you sell more in summer? In winter? Tell whether your products will be available only during certain times of the year, or if you will offer **alternate** products or services. Your business might provide lawn mowing in summer, and snow removal in winter.

Explain how existing **competition** might effect your sales. Tell how you meet the customers' needs better than your competitor. For example, are your prices lower or is your product of higher quality? Do you have more promotions? List any special features your product or service offers.

Business Plan: Finances

Income projection statement
(profit-loss statement) January 2003 - De...

	Jan.	Feb.	Mar.	Apr.	May	Jun.	Jul.	Aug.
Total sales (revenues)								
Costs of sales								
Gross profit								
Gross profit margin								
Variable expenses								
Salaries								
Advertising								

Financial Statements
Barker's Biscuits balance sheet as of March 1, 2003

Assets	Cash on hand	$_____
	Money due from customers	$_____
	Value of inventory	$_____
	Value of business and office equipment	$_____
	Total assets	$_____
	...ey owed to customers	$_____
	...ey owed to suppliers	$_____
	...n payment	

April 1, 2003–June 30, 2003 Cash Flow continued . . .

| | April | M... |
	est.	act.	est.
5. Cash paid out			
(a) Purchases (merchandise)			
(b) Outside services			
(c) Supplies (office and operating)			
(d) Car, delivery, and travel			
(e) Rent			
(f) Telephone, utilities			
(g) Taxes (income, ect.)			
(h) Loan payment			
(i) Equipment rental			
3. Total cash paid out (5a+5i)			
4. Cash on hand at end of month (4 - 6)			

Barker's Biscuits
Monthly Cash Flow Projection
April 1, 2003–June 30, 2003

	April		May		June		Total	
	est.	act.	est.	act.	est.	act.	est.	act.
1. Cash on hand (beginning of month)								
2. Cash taken in								
(a) Cash sales								
(b) Cash paid on credit accounts								
(c) Money received from loans								
3. Total cash receipts (2a+2b+2c=3)								
4. Total cash available (1+3)								

Many reference books, workbooks, and Internet sources can help you prepare financial statements.

The **finance** portion of the business plan should detail your financial hopes for the business. It should list the **assets** of the business. Assets include the amount of cash on hand, the amount of money owed to the business, and the value of everything—supplies and equipment— owned by the business.

This section also lists the **liabilities** of the business. Liabilities include all the **debts, loans,** and other financial obligations of a business. A business's assets minus its liabilities equals the **net worth** of the business.

An **income projection** statement, also known as a **profit** and loss statement, should be in this part of the business plan. The statement

Assets – Liabilities = Net Worth

shows how much the business takes in and how much it pays out in expenses. Businesses pay two kinds of expenses: fixed expenses and variable expenses. Fixed expenses are expenses that are the same every month and may include rent, insurance premiums, and loan payments.

Variable expenses, sometimes called controllable expenses, are expenses that may be different from one month to the next. Variable expenses may include salaries, advertising, electricity bill, and office supplies.

Finally, a monthly cash flow projection should be included in the business plan. This statement tells how much cash the business takes in during a month and how much cash the business pays out during the same month.

Eighteen and under

Being both an **entrepreneur** and under age eighteen has disadvantages. Dan Finley, owner of The View, a website that reviews computer hardware, comments: "You can't sign contracts, can't get a credit card; every bank account you have has to have a parent's name on it."

Yet, being underage can give young entrepreneurs an edge. Dr. Marilyn Kourilsky, who has studied teen entrepreneurs points out, "I'm sure [people] thought Bill Gates was adorable. It's very hard to say no to a kid."

This picture shows Bill Gates as a teen. He began his first business venture when he was fifteen years old. He founded Microsoft Corporation at age nineteen.

Business Plan: Management

The management section of a business plan identifies the owners of the business, as well as any key employees. It presents information about each person's education, volunteer experience, and work experience. Any special skills or experience should be stressed. If one partner or employee has experience in sales, while another has special computer skills, these individuals' skills should be mentioned here.

dog biscuits

Recipe

Dear Aunt Min,

Thank you for your help in preparing the business plan for Barker's. Thank you, too, for the advice about weighing ingredients rather than measuring them. We are glad you're around to answer any questions we have about the baking part of the business. As always, your chocobars are the best!

Love, Susan

Management

Susan Hanover Operations Director
Tianna Madison Sales Director
Miriam Hanover Advisor
Owner/operator Red Hen Bakery (four years)
Bud Hanover Advisor
Partner, Groomindale's Dog Care Salon
Marcus and Irma Madison Advisors
Owners, Madison Gifts, Roscoe, Sheffield, and Main Street locations

If you are the only person involved in the business, include information about anyone who might help you make business decisions or provide advice. Tell what strengths they add to the business, and how you will use them as well as how often. This is also the place to mention if you use the services of an attorney, a small business **consultant,** or the local Small Business Administration office.

Job hunting

Early in 2000, seventeen-year-old Saied Ghafari had a bright idea. Create a website targeting teen job seekers and pay for it with advertising from companies looking to hire those same teens. The idea was the result of Ghafari's frustration in finding a decent summer job. "I went to every single site and nothing came up. So I thought, 'Why don't I create a site so teens can come and find jobs?'" Ghafari did not find a job—he "found" a business.

Ghafari had the support and help of family members. His mom took a leave of absence from her job to research the market **potential** of Ghafari's online project. In addition, his uncle's web design company created the site, saving the teen thousands of dollars. The site has collected **revenues** from companies such as Coca-Cola, Banana Republic, and First Virginia Bank.

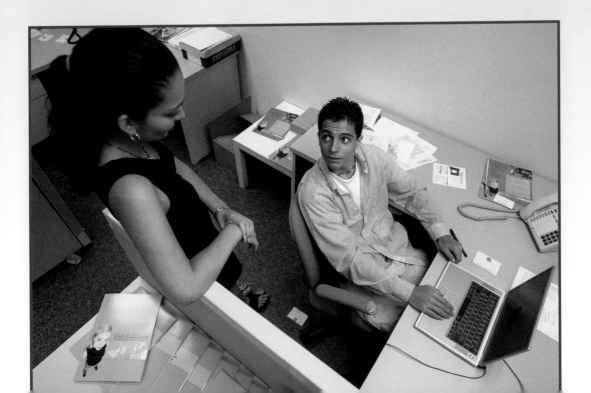

Business Plan: Operations

Meet once a week to compare "To do" lists. Discuss results and problems

To Do

Susan	Tianna
Develop recipes	Test recipes
Order baking supplies	Order business and advertising supplies
Bake biscuits using family kitchen ovens	Package and distribute biscuits for sale
Hours: variable day or night according to availability	Marketing (analyze competition, distribute samples)
20 hours/week	Record keeping
"To Do" List	Hours: variable days according to store hours
	20 hours/week
	"To Do" List

dog biscuits

Recipe

Operations

Susan Hanover Operations Director

- Develop recipes
- Order baking supplies
- Bake biscuits using family kitchen ovens
  Hours: variable–day or night according to kitchen availability;
  20 hrs/week
- Weekly To Do list
- Weekly Partner Meeting

Operations

Tianna Madison Sales Director

- Test recipes
- Order business and advertising supplies
- Package & distribute biscuits for sale
- Marketing (analyze competition, distribute samples)
- Record keeping
- Hours: variable–days according to specialty store hours;
  20 hrs/week
- Weekly To Do list
- Weekly Partner Meeting

If you have a partner or employees, you will need to list their specific responsibilities.

This section should give an **overview** of how day-to-day business will be handled. In order to write the overview, it may be best to list the **operational** details of the business. Who will make the product or deliver the **service?** How will you insure the quality of your product or service? What special arrangements with people or other businesses have been made to help start the business?

At age fifteen, a business idea began to simmer in Maleka Lenzy's mind. During a NFTE program for teens, she learned to write a business plan and started a catering company. In the beginning, Lenzy sold gift baskets and barbecue at flea markets and trade shows. Soon her business, Classy Productions, began to hear from larger clients. Business **revenues** went from $2,000 the first year to more than $2,000 a month after two years. As a college student, Lenzy limits her Classy Productions activities to summer break. After graduation, Lenzy plans to run the business full time.

The day-to-day operations of the business should be considered as well. For example, will you work weekends but not weekdays? Work some days but not others? How many hours per day or per week do you expect to work? How many hours do you expect your partner or employees to work? Do you drive yourself or do you rely on others for transportation? Who is responsible for ordering equipment and supplies?

Successful **entrepreneurs** often write up schedules, procedures, and guidelines for the business and then test them for a week or two. In some cases, a schedule may need to be adjusted or guidelines may need to be changed.

Above all, there should be written guidelines telling how to handle differences and disagreements among partners, managers, and employees.

Know It

Schedules and guidelines describing how a business operates go a long way to ensuring that the business operates smoothly and with as few problems as possible.

THIS NOTE
FOR ALL DEBT

Business Plan: Appendix

The appendix is the place in a business plan to include information that may be too detailed for other parts of the plan. It may also include information that is not directly related to the plan, but helps explain parts of the plan.

For example, the appendix is the place to present any sample marketing or sales materials you have. Here, too, is the place for photographs of the product, as well as copies of flyers, ads for local newspapers, and designs for stationery, business cards, or packaging. Include details of the market research you completed and any appropriate newspaper or magazine articles.

Add to Appendix:
- Mention Mr. and Mrs. Madison's store and Tianna's work there.
- Mention Aunt Min and her successful bakery and Susan's work there.
- Include Bud's successful dog grooming business
- Show drawings of logo
- Include copies of market research articles from Internet

Bud's first grooming customer

Appendix

About the Owners:

Susan Hanover is a ninth-grader at Westlake High School where she has a 3.8 grade average. She has worked the past three summers at the Red Hen Bakery learning how to measure, mix, prepare, and decorate a variety of baked goods. In 2003, Susan won first place in General Flour's Junior Bake-Off.

Tianna Madison is a ninth-grader at Westlake High School where she has a 3.9 grade average. She has worked after school and during summers as cashier at Madison's Gifts where she gained experience in ordering, stocking, and bookkeeping. In 2003, Tianna was captain of the state champion Westlake girl's volleyball team.

As a new business, it may be helpful to include your **resume** as well as the resumes of your partner(s), any employees, and people who will be helping you make business decisions.

If you are presenting the business plan as part of a **loan** or grant application, you may need to include your credit history, copies of leases, licenses, and contracts in the appendix.

Generation Y

Amber Sade Bundy, of East Palo Alto, California, started Khinde & Ndosi Fashion Consulting (K & N) to provide market research to local retailers on the fashion preferences of young women between the ages of 13 and 22 (also known as Generation Y). "Retailers need to see the buying **potential** of my community and to recognize their preferences and specific needs."

Amber has developed a nine-step approach to identifying potential clients and analyzing their needs. She formed a focus group of her peers to provide data on product selection to local merchants. Amber intends to expand K & N by starting a website offering customized clothing at affordable prices.

"I feel so strongly about my business and the potential for its success that I have made it my top priority."

Start-up Costs

Barker's Biscuit Start-up costs

Ingredients:
flour and other raw materials

Equipment:
spoons, bowls, scrapers, scale,
mixer, etc. $350

Kitchen rental:

Supplies: $450
pens, pencils, paper, receipt books, $10/month
bookkeeping notebook/journal

Packaging Supplies:
bags, stick-on labels
(1,000 minimum) $50

City license:

Insurance: $200

Advertising: $50
Flyers, photocopying costs $0

Design:
Assistance in designing logo $150

                                                   $150

the competiti[on]

New! Dog Treats $5

A start-up budget is a combination of
research and estimation. Many businesses
fail because they do not have enough money
for start-up expenses.

Some would-be **entrepreneurs** feel that
estimating their start-up costs is a bit like
using a dictionary to find out how to spell
a word. They say, "I can't know what I'll
need until I'll need it."

A start-up budget should include
amounts for the following:
- rent
- licenses/permits
- equipment
- insurance
- supplies
- advertising
- legal fees
- employee **wages**
- utilities.

Luckily, there are guidelines to help an entrepreneur estimate his or her start-up costs. For example, the business needs a place "to be." Will there be rent to pay? Are there deposits for electricity and telephone?

The business will need supplies such as receipt books, pens, pencils, and perhaps a telephone and a computer to run efficiently. In addition, the business will need equipment to do its actual business. For example, a bicycle repair business will need equipment such as screwdrivers, wrenches, tire plugs, and spray paint. The start-up budget should allow for these expenses.

The business should also have enough money on hand to cover **operating** expenses for a few months or even a year. These expenses include your salary and money to repay any **loans.**

If you need a loan, the bank or lender will probably ask:
- How will you use the loan?
- How much do you need to borrow?
- How will you repay the loan?

You will need to give them a clear business plan, including **financial** statements, business goals, description of your experience and management capabilities, as well as the expertise of other key employees.

The 2nd Gear budget

Teen entrepreneur Jason Upshaw, from Cambridge, Massachusetts, owns 2nd Gear Bicycles. He began the business when he was fifteen. Now nineteen, Jason credits his success to help from Boston Youth Venture. Jason says that when he started his bike shop, getting enough money was important. He had to make sure that he had a good working space and the proper tools.

"When I submitted my first budget, it was the most unsure thing I had ever put before someone else. Everything is an estimate, especially if it's your first time putting a budget together."

"Estimating what I was going to spend over the next six months was very difficult. I just stuck to the costs I knew like rent and tools. Things like telephone, heating, electric, and supply costs were all unknowns to me."

Pricing

An anxious teen may just name a price for the business's product without knowing if the price is right. A wise teen will figure out the price of one item, also called a unit price. The overall goal is to find a price that will more than cover the cost and will compare well with the **competitors'** price.

To find the best price, you will need to find the cost of one unit. For example, if the product is T-shirts, the unit of sale is one T-shirt, the unit price is the selling price of one T-shirt, and the unit cost is the cost of producing one T-shirt.

The cost of producing a product depends on three factors: the cost of **raw materials** needed to produce the product, the cost of labor needed to produce the product, and the cost of **overhead**. If your business sells more than one product, you will need to find the unit cost for each of the products.

The key to calculating the cost of sales is to not overlook any costs. Be sure to include the cost of moving your product from where you make it to where you will sell it. If you are providing a **service** at a customer's location, you will need to include your transportation cost.

Once you know the cost per unit, you are ready to determine the price per unit.

As you make your product, you will find that some things must be replaced for each unit you make. That is, you will need to replace the paint used for T-shirts or the flour used for dog biscuits. Other items will last for hundreds or even thousands of units. For example, both the mixing buckets for paints or cookie sheets for dog biscuits will last for several hundred units. You will need to **estimate** the cost per unit of these items and include that cost in your calculations.

Barker's Biscuit cost per unit
(unit = 1 dozen cookies)

Goods needed to produce biscuits	Cost	Number of units	Cost for one unit (12 cookies)
Ingredients (flour, eggs, flavor) 1.25		1	$1.05
Mixer $240.00 good for 5,000 units $240		5,000	0.05
8 mixing bowls, should last for 5,000 units $48		5,000	0.0096
10 cookie sheets and racks, should be good for 5,000 units $59		5,000	0.018
Wooden spoons and rubber scrapers, replace every 1,000 units ... $12		1,000	0.012
Oven mitts, towels should last for 2,000 units $18		2,000	0.009
Cleaning supplies for about 500 units $20		500	0.10
Paper bags and labels, 1000 ....$23		1000	0.23
Kitchen rental, one month or about 1000 units $10		1000	0.01
Advertising for 1,000 units $18		2000	0.018
Total cost per unit $1.51			

Do you want your price to match the competition's price? Do you want to price your product significantly lower than the competition? Once you choose a price, be sure to check that the price per unit is greater than your cost per unit. The difference between your cost per unit and the price per unit is the gross **profit** per unit.

> **Price per unit**
> **– Cost per unit**
> ─────────────────
> **Gross profit per unit**

Be careful not to think of this number as profit because it is not. Up to now, your figures have included only the cost of making the product—T-shirts—not the expense of doing business—advertising, utilities, salaries, and so on. To find the profit, you will need to subtract the expense of doing business from the gross profit.

Another number useful in tracking how well your business is doing is the gross profit margin.

Gross Profit Margin = [(Gross profits) ÷ (Total net sales)] x 100%

Record Keeping

Many young **entrepreneurs** find it difficult to keep accurate and up-to-date business records. They feel the task is uninteresting and unnecessary. They do not realize that accurate records showing the **income** and costs of the business can help a business owner keep costs low and sell the business's goods or **services** for more.

Three factors can help young entrepreneurs set up a good record-keeping system. The system should be simple, accurate, and timely. Keeping records does not have to involve difficult accounting principles. With no more than an ordinary notebook, a young entrepreneur can begin record keeping. Records of sales, money received from customers, money owed by customers, and money used for business purchases are essential.

> ## Know It
>
> Every business needs an accurate description of its **profit** in order to pay **federal income** taxes.

The amounts recorded in the notebook come from receipts associated with the business. A receipt is a record of expense. Each type of receipt should be kept in its own folder. For example, one folder can hold the sales receipts written as customers make a purchase. When you sell your product or service, you must always give the customer a receipt. Each sales receipt should show the amount of the purchase, how much the customer paid, and how much remains to be paid. The totals from these receipts are recorded in the *sales, money received from customers,* and *money owed by customers* portions of the notebook.

If a customer does not pay for a product or service when it is received, you will bill the customer at a later date. The bill is also called an invoice. Record the amount of the invoice as *money owed by customers.* When the customer pays the bill, mark the invoice "paid" and record the amount as *money received from customer.* Keep invoices ordered by number or alphabetized by customer name so that you can easily locate them.

Another folder can hold the receipts the business owner receives each time he or she makes a purchase for the business. Always get a receipt for each purchase you make for the business. The totals from these receipts are recorded in the *money used for business* portion of the notebook. Be sure to save the receipts until tax time—business owners may deduct many of their expenses from the taxes they owe, but they must have the receipts to prove the expenses.

A Wonderful Party
2102 Division Street
Roscoe, Illinois
March 1, 2003

8 party hats	.$16
bibs	.$2
16 balloons	.$8
paper candy cups	.$4
Total	.$30
Received	.$30

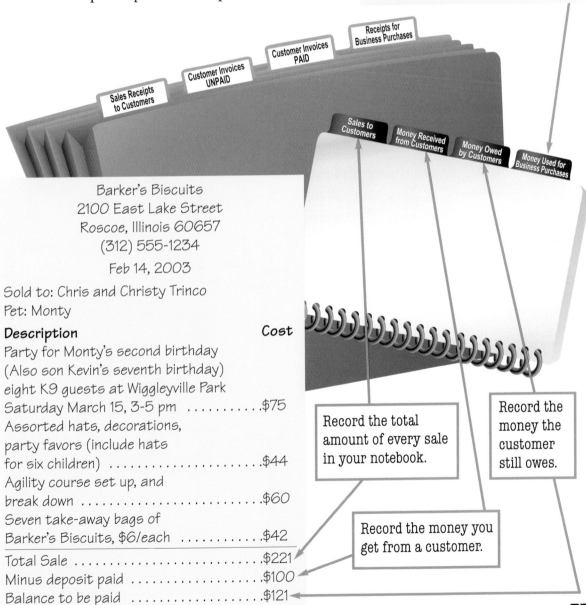

Barker's Biscuits
2100 East Lake Street
Roscoe, Illinois 60657
(312) 555-1234

Feb 14, 2003

Sold to: Chris and Christy Trinco
Pet: Monty

Description	Cost
Party for Monty's second birthday (Also son Kevin's seventh birthday) eight K9 guests at Wiggleyville Park Saturday March 15, 3-5 pm	.$75
Assorted hats, decorations, party favors (include hats for six children)	.$44
Agility course set up, and break down	.$60
Seven take-away bags of Barker's Biscuits, $6/each	.$42
Total Sale	.$221
Minus deposit paid	.$100
Balance to be paid	.$121

Record the total amount of every sale in your notebook.

Record the money the customer still owes.

Record the money you get from a customer.

37

Profit and Loss

Every business owner or manager needs to prepare a **profit** and loss statement, also called an **income** statement, at least once a year. The statement tells whether the business made a profit or experienced a loss during the time covered by the statement.

Preparing a monthly profit and loss statement can help a young **entrepreneur** tell if the business is meeting the **financial projections** made in the business plan. Business owners can use the statement to compare business performance from one time period to another. If there is a big change in **net income**, the statement may help show what parts of the business were responsible for the change.

The "bottom line" refers to the last line on a profit and loss statement. This is the line that tells whether the company has made a profit or experienced a loss.

To buy a computer or not

Deciding whether or not a business needs a computer requires a clear understanding of the advantages and disadvantages involved. A computer can help keep track of inventory, sales, suppliers, and customers as well as aid in financial record keeping. The key is knowing what kind of system, and which software, best suits your business. A poorly chosen computer, or software that is too difficult to use, can be a great disadvantage.

A profit and loss statement gives a picture of a business's financial health during a specific time period.

This number includes the amount of money actually collected, as well as the money customers owe for **services** or products they purchased during March 2003.

Barker's Biscuits
Profit And Loss Statement
(March 2003)

Income

1. Money received from customers or owed by customers _____

2. Refunds to customers _____

3. Money on hand (line 1 less line 2) _____

Expenses _____

4. The cost of items or services sold. _____

5. Wages paid to employees. _____

6. Interest on loans made to company. _____

7. Purchases made for business. _____

8. Total expenses (sum of lines 4 to 7) _____

9. Total net income (line 3 less line 8). _____

Any time you give a customer a refund, you must subtract it from the amount on line 1.

Any purchase for the business—even one that will be paid for later—should be recorded here.

This is the per-unit cost of the product or services multiplied by the number of items sold or hours billed. Costs, such as transportation or storage fees, per unit should be included in this number.

THIS NOTE
FOR ALL DEBT

Laws and Taxes

In addition to the market research needed for a business plan, a new business owner must also research what **federal,** state, county, and city government laws might affect the business.

For example, any time you work for someone else, or for yourself, you must have a **social security number.** If a young **entrepreneur's** business has a **profit** greater than $400 in a year, he or she must file a tax return. If a business has employees, the business owner will need to set aside part of the employees' pay for federal and state **income** taxes, as well as contributions to the employees' social security. This is true throughout the United States.

To get a social security number you will need an original or certified version of your birth certificate plus some other form of identification like a baptismal record. Bring the identification to a nearby office of the Social Security Administration.

United We Wear

United We Wear

September 11, 2001, deeply affected eleven-year-old David Parkinson of New York City. He decided to make and sell hand-beaded American flag pins and patriotic bookmarks. "I didn't start the business to make a quick profit. I decided that I would donate twenty percent of every sale to two local firehouses, which lost a combined twenty firefighters." David also donated money from his sales to his school's annual educational trip, since many of the students could not afford to go.

"I am committed to helping my community through my business."

In addition, some cities and states require a license for certain businesses such as dog grooming, street performer, or bicycle messenger. Many cities require that businesspeople get a peddler's license before they sell their products on the street or at malls.

Entrepreneurs also need to be aware of **patents** and **trademarks.** For example, Binney & Smith hold the patent for Silly Putty.™ So, no one other than Binney & Smith can manufacture Silly Putty.™ In addition, the name "Silly Putty" is a registered trademark. No one, other than Binney & Smith, can use the name "Silly Putty" for any product he or she might manufacture.

If a young entrepreneur has invented a new-to-the-world product, he or she should talk to a lawyer about getting a patent for the invention. And, if an entrepreneur uses a special logo or catchy phrase for the product or **service**, that phrase or logo should be registered as a trademark.

Every business must have a Federal Identification Number. If you are the business owner and there are no employees, you can usually use your social security number.

Many of today's most popular products are known by their trademarked names rather than their descriptive names such as cola, gelatin desert, or crayon.

The Form of the Company

Young **entrepreneurs** may not give much thought to the type of company that they will run. Often they jump right in, assuming they will own and operate their business by themselves. Sometimes two or three young entrepreneurs will work together to run a business. A smart businessperson, however, knows the advantages and disadvantages of each type of company.

A business that has only one owner who is also the manager is a sole proprietorship. Usually, it is the easiest company structure to operate. A sole proprietorship always requires a **social security number.** Sometimes, depending on the location and the type of business, it may also require a business registration and a business license.

Know It

Most young entrepreneurs form businesses that are either sole proprietorships or partnerships.

The **sole proprietor** is the only boss and has total authority to manage the business **operations.** Decisions can be made quickly, without consulting any one else. However, because there is only one boss, that boss is responsible for all the business's problems. For example, if the product or **service** offered by a sole proprietor injures a customer, the sole proprietor is responsible for paying any costs associated with the injury.

If two or more people agree to share ownership, and sometimes management, of a business, that business is a partnership. In a partnership, each partner can make business decisions. Of course, having more partners means more bosses, so it often takes longer to make decisions.

Entrepreneurs should consider what kinds of things a partner might contribute to the business. An entrepreneur should evaluate a **potential** partner's values, work ethic, and work experience. A friend should be a partner only if he or she will really help the business grow.

Because there are more people responsible for running the business, all the work does not fall on any one person. If the product or service injures a customer, each of the partners is responsible for paying any costs associated with the injury.

There is another type of company organization—the corporation. In general, corporations are expensive and time consuming to operate. Corporations must follow many government regulations. Therefore, few young entrepreneurs choose this form of business.

Franchises

Many of the nation's brand-name hamburger, sandwich, and pizza restaurants are actually small businesses. Most of these businesses are franchises. In a franchise arrangement, an entrepreneur and an established successful business work together. For a fee, the established business provides guidelines for producing the successful product—such as hamburgers or pizza. The entrepreneur must follow the guidelines so that every location offers exactly the same product.

Common Mistakes

A few common mistakes are responsible for thousands of business failures. However, many of these mistakes can be avoided if an **entrepreneur** is careful.

Many entrepreneurs fail to recognize all the business's costs. For instance, teens who start lawn-mowing businesses tend to use their family's lawn mower. If the teen does not include the cost of servicing the mower, then the **profit** figures for the business are not accurate. Small expenses can add up to big numbers and should be included in the cost of their product or **service**.

Teens in business

The Bureau of Labor Statistics and other organizations that study entrepreneurship have found that:

70 percent of high school seniors want to go into business for themselves

12–14 percent of all teen businesses are still in business after high school

85 percent of teens want to learn more about starting their own business

10 percent of new businesses are started by people under age 25

Some entrepreneurs spend all of the money they take in from selling their product or service. They think of this money as profit. They forget that to find true profit, they need to subtract all their expenses—including the money they borrowed or used for start–up—from the money they take in.

There are many foundations, non-profit organizations, and others that are willing to **fund** a variety of projects or businesses. When you apply for money from this type of organization, be sure you know what kinds of businesses received money in the past. This may help you as you fill out the application forms. Above all, pay attention to deadlines. Start writing your proposal two or three weeks before the deadline. And remember, a clear business plan will go far in helping you explain your new business idea.

In their eagerness to make their business work, some teens may take on too many customers. These teens may have decided how much money they want to make and how many customers they will need to reach their goal. Unfortunately, the number of customers is often too great for the new business to handle. The teens find they do not have enough time to make enough product or provide enough service to meet all of their customers' demands.

Other mistakes to watch out for include starting a business that totally depends on physical strength, or not being able to manage the time necessary for school, homework, recreation, family obligations, and the business.

There are several actions you can take to help your adult customers place their trust in a young entrepreneur.

- Design a logo for your business and use it on everything possible. If at all possible, print your business cards and any stationery in color.
- Give yourself a title such as Director or Vice President. This will help give you the respect, as well as give the impression of being part of a larger company. Do not broadcast that you are the only one in the company.
- Always answer your telephone with a professional voice. If possible, purchase a professional voice mail service.

Glossary

alternate to do or perform by turns

asset total value of a company or thing; property that can be used to pay debts

brochure booklet explaining a business

competition business offering similar product or service

consultant person who gives professional advice

debt something that is owed

economy use or management of money; system for managing, production, distribution, and sales of goods and services

entrepreneur person who starts a business

estimation informed guess

federal describing a union of states that share a government

finance money matter

firm business company, usually consisting of several people

flexibility ability to adapt to new or changing requirements

fund finance or pay for

income money earned through work

innovation change in the usual way of doing things

liability debt or financial obligation

loan money given to a borrower, to be repaid with interest

long-term long period of time, such as years

minimum wage lowest wage payable by law

net income business's total earnings, minus costs of doing business, interest, taxes, and other expenses

net worth total assets minus total liabilities

operation action taken to keep a business working

overhead general business expenses, such as lighting, rent, and heating

overview broad view

patent government grant giving a business (or person) the exclusive right to sell an invention

potential possible

projection estimate of what will happen

profit money made in a business venture; gain from a business after costs are subtracted from money taken in

raw material material in its natural state used in producing manufactured goods

resume summary of a person's work, school, and volunteer experience

revenue money coming in; income

service work done for another or others

social security number number assigned by the government to track income for pensions and medical care

sole proprietor person who owns and runs a business by himself or herself

short-term short period of time, such as weeks

strategy plan for a business's future

trademark mark, symbol, or similar registered with the government and used by a manufacturer to identify a product

trillion one thousand billions

wage payment for work based on the number of hours worked or the rate of production

More Books to Read

Burkett, Larry (ed.). *Money Matters for Kids.* Chicago: Moody Press, 2001.

Giesecke, Ernestine. *Managing Your Money.* Chicago: Heinemann Library, 2003.

Macht, Norman. *Money and Banking.* Broomall, Penn.: Chelsea House, 2001.

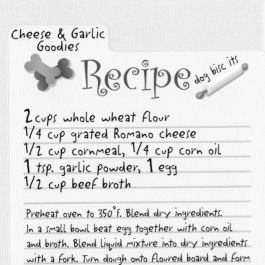

Cheese & Garlic Goodies

Recipe — dog biscuits

2 cups whole wheat flour
1/4 cup grated Romano cheese
1/2 cup cornmeal, 1/4 cup corn oil
1 tsp. garlic powder, 1 egg
1/2 cup beef broth

Preheat oven to 350°F. Blend dry ingredients. In a small bowl beat egg together with corn oil and broth. Blend liquid mixture into dry ingredients with a fork. Turn dough onto floured board and form a ball. Roll to 1/3" thickness. Cut biscuits into shapes. Place on oiled cookie sheet. Bake for 30 minutes.

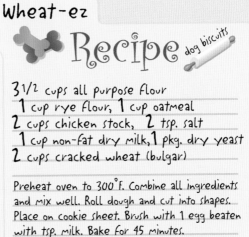

Wheat-ez

Recipe — dog biscuits

3 1/2 cups all purpose flour
1 cup rye flour, 1 cup oatmeal
2 cups chicken stock, 2 tsp. salt
1 cup non-fat dry milk, 1 pkg. dry yeast
2 cups cracked wheat (bulgar)

Preheat oven to 300°F. Combine all ingredients and mix well. Roll dough and cut into shapes. Place on cookie sheet. Brush with 1 egg beaten with tsp. milk. Bake for 45 minutes.

Index